LEARNING CURVE

AN INTRODUCTION TO (DEATH ROW INMATE) JOHNNY D. MILES' COLLAGE ART, POETRY & MIND

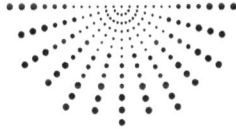

JOHNNY DUANE MILES

TIO MACDONALD

X
EAST
OAKLAND

"Understanding Positivity":

Father Freed is a positive man now in God's bosom. He is like a guardian angel for those that have hidden hurts. His message is 'Peace!'

This book is dedicated to the life of Father Eric Freed. Eric Freed is a martyr for the culture of life. He was murdered in California, in 2014. He was a beloved priest for many of the Catholic Christian Faith.

A collage dedicated to Father Eric Freed can be found at www. milesdynasty.com

MILES DYNASTY

All poems and collage overviews found in *The Johnny Duane Miles' Learning Curve* are inspired by and explain Johnny Miles' original collage art available for free viewing and download at the website: www.milesdynasty.com

The East Oakland Times encourages viewing the collages while reading and/or listening to the content of *Learning Curve*.

INTRODUCTION

Nancy Willem, a rape crisis counselor, by murder died February 4, 1992. In her Rialto California office, Nancy Willem was raped, robbed, and brutally beaten. Nancy Willem courageously fought against her attacker, causing injuries resulting in blood evidence. Analyzed blood samples were alleged to match the rare blood type of Johnny Duane Miles who had been apprehended in Torrance, California for an office robbery and rape. The County of San Bernardino condemned to death Johnny Duane Miles for the murder, rape, and robbery of Nancy Willem. In Los Angeles County, Johnny Duane Miles was sentenced to 75 years and eight months for rape and robbery.

Johnny Miles is a black American man primarily raised in the neighborhoods of Compton, in Southern California. In the 1980s, Compton became known nationally for dangerous streets and the gangster rap group NWA (Niggas with Attitudes.) Regarding Johnny Mile's mental health, during the San Bernardino trial, clinical psychologist Joseph A. Lantz reported that Johnny Miles suffered from bizarre and paranoid delusions. Deputy Public Defender

Joseph Canty stated that "Mr. (Johnny) Miles is actively psychotic" (Brooks, B4.) In 2018, The National Association for the Advancement of Colored People (NAACP) presented to the California Supreme Court prejudicial concerns regarding jury selection in the San Bernardino trial against Johnny Miles.

Case related statements are based in the following newspaper articles. No court records were accessed:

1. Patrick J. McDonnell. "Tests Link Ex-Convict to Rapes and Murder." *Los Angeles Times/Washington Edition,* Thursday, June 25, 1992, p. B4.

2. Richard Brooks. "Attorney doubts client's sanity." *The San Bernardino County Sun,* Friday, March 20, 1998, p. B4.

3. Bob Egelko and Megan Cassidy. "'O.J. strategy': Lawyers say prosecutors ask about guilt to cull black jurors." *San Francisco Chronicle,* Sunday, November 4, 2018

* * *

Twenty-seven years after the murder of Nancy Willem, the State of California has not put Johnny Miles to death. For the majority of the past twenty-seven years, Johnny Miles has lived in a one-person cell on San Quentin's death row, among hundreds of others convicted of first-degree murder. Johnny Miles has had to find a measure of acceptance to continue living on death row. He has not chosen suicide or to use hard drugs. Neither has he been a victim of a fatal attack by other inmates. Johnny Miles has chosen to live while under the sentence of death.

Johnny Miles is the primary author of the book: ***THE JOHNNY D. MILES LEARNING CURVE: An Introduction to (Death Row Inmate) Johnny D. Miles' Collage Art, Poetry & Mind***. The title communicates the intent of the book. The book is an introduction and guide to Johnny Miles inspiration, imagination, inner-thoughts, and emotions as expressed through his collage art, collage explanations, and poetry.

I, Tio MacDonald, am the founder of the East Oakland Times (EOT) and the producer and chief editor of the My Crime Series, a series of biographies written by inmates, on inmates. The My Crime series proposes to "candidly communicate the upbringing, life experience, character, and motivations of the incarcerated." The purpose of such communication is to grant the broader public an understanding of the men and women in California prisons (www.crimebios.com)

Learning Curve, of which I am the co-author, has a similar intent to that of the My Crime Series, to communicate to the public, the character, inspiration, motivations, psychology, and mental processes of California death row inmate, Johnny Duane Miles. Whereas the My Crime books are short, engaging biographical narratives, *Learning Curve* is abstract, allusion rather than explanation forms the heart of the book's communication; at the same time, *Learning Curve* is richer in explorations of the existential and identity processed through the condition of incarceration.

Learning Curve is fine art in that patient informed perception is required for a fuller imbuing of Johnny Mile's artistic intent and subterranean self-expression. *Learning Curve* is meant for the learned: a person that can separate flair from meaning; a person able to perceive thematic repetition and aberration; more or less an investigative and curious art enthusiast and/or enjoyer of abstract poetry.

Learning Curve is meant for the coffee table, next to the Rubik's Cube. Both offer the complexity of a puzzle and the satisfaction of completion. I propose that persons interested in fine arts, poetics, and psychology will find the most interest and profit from *Learning Curve*.

Johnny Mile's collaging and poetry exist within the solitary confinement of his own sense of rhyme and rhythm, concept, tone, and intrigue. His work is a soliloquy in the effort to find meaning and transmit meaning. All reading of his work should occur with the background knowledge of his minimal formal education for Johnny dropped out of school in the 10th grade.

* * *

My reason for suggesting a book to Johnny Miles was for the artistic appreciation and psychological insight that the learned may achieve. From his own impetuses, Johnny presented his collage art to me. In our phone interactions, I perceived unique manners of articulation indicating mental processes worthy of understanding. I thought Johnny's art offered an inroad to his psyche, meaning his thinking, inspiration, motivations (self-interest), values, and knowledge of self in isolation and in a community, death row. Further, I held his collage work to be exceptional and worthy of broader cognizance.

This book, *Learning Curve*, inspires Johnny Miles. Since we began the creation and assemblage of collages and writings for the book, Johnny has taken up study to improve his skill as a writer. Additionally, I provided Johnny with educational materials by which he could further understand the concepts that make up the visual arts, such as space, repetition, theme, point of view, etc.

The word psychopath denoted is clinical while in general parlance communicates pure evil. The word "psychopathy" connotes less negativity to the labeled while still bordering on insult. Basketball great Michael Jordan has been called psychopathic as has the sitting American President, Donald Trump. British psychologist Kevin Dutton in his so-called, "Great British Psychopath Survey" found many eminently valued professions, such as clergy, filled in great proportions by psychopaths. Due to my own lack of credentials and my genuine relationship with Johnny Miles I cannot label him. However,

Johnny Mile's art and poetic expressions are a step toward Johnny Miles exposing himself to the world as he is.

My request of Johnny and hope is that as we work together for the creation and promotion of *Learning Curve* and future books, that he finds the highest value in a sincere exposition of self. *Learning Curve* offers Johnny Miles today. He is alive and has purpose. The Johnny Miles of tomorrow, I pray, for society's benefit and his own, will be more fully conscious of the good he can further deliver by revealing greater depths and insight into the ranges of his self-knowledge, past and present.

* * *

Men on death row generally do not want their execution. I say this based on my relationships with more than twenty women and men on California's death row. Of this number, I have had numerous in-person meetings. My overall relationship with inmates in more than five California Department of Corrections and Rehabilitation (CDCR) prisons is extensive. My 2018 winter holiday letter included over 120 people. In 2018, I spent seven and a quarter 40-hour work weeks talking on the phone with inmates in California prisons. I have been engaged with inmates in a non-professional capacity, I have never worked or received any money from the state, for three busy years.

My purpose in initiating these relationships began in a desire to be a catalyst for change in East Oakland, the predominantly black and Hispanic American neighborhood of Oakland, California. For over ten years, my intermittent work as an instructor brought me to East Oakland, an area categorized as impoverished and highly dangerous.

I worked at many reentry centers in Oakland including the Salvation Army and Men of Valor. Additionally, I taught at Castlemont High

School, Youth Uprising, and the now-defunct Edward Shands Adult School, all located in the heart of deep East Oakland.

What I perceived in Oakland was buckets being used by the school district, non-profits, and government agencies to remove an ocean of difficulties levied against achieving a healthy community. The teachers I worked with were dedicated, gifted, and experienced and undoubtedly made incredible impacts on young people. However, I perceived that top-down tactics are not achieving community health. I believe that the community of East Oakland will need to figure out for themselves how to use government resources and to fight against political roadblocks for addressing and lessening communal and systematic suffering.

I intended to make myself valuable to the black American community of East Oakland. I began attending church in East Oakland. I made a point of visiting the streets and allowing for natural interactions. I posted self-promoting flyers. Outside of the library, McDonald's, and a few friendly and good time bars, for me, there is not a lot to do. Safety is a concern. Skid Row in East Oakland is permanent, and even for the passer-by, there are never dreamt of sights. My beginnings were exploratory, and my real self-promotion began after the East Oakland Times produced short stories written by inmates to be distributed on the streets of East Oakland. The premier edition was called, "Rehabilitation." The purpose of the stories was for promoting EOT to East Oakland, the advocation of life culture, and offering street-level messages of care and concern, from those who know ghetto life to those who are living it.

Johnny Miles grew up in the equally impoverished and dangerous streets of Compton. He was an adolescent at the height of the Los Angeles gang epidemic. He grew up where punches are thrown, knives are used, and guns are shot. He lived where crack cocaine was born and bled out black American neighborhoods. He knows the dissipation that results from discarded needles, bottles, and pipes.

These descriptions of black American inner-city life have been heard countless times before. When we admit that the inner-city black American has been left to cultural death and actual death, we can call ourselves honest. We know this as much as we know not to visit the black American inner-city. We know this as much as we know that the consistent homicides found in Section B of the daily newspaper will not end. We know this as much as we condone black American teens being convicted and sentenced to a lifetime in prison for street-level crimes. We know this when reading that abortion rates in black American communities exceed birth rates. The black American inner-city is a meme to Americans who do not know it. There are crying mothers, angry gangsters, and shepherd-like pastors trying to move black Americans in the direction of "Never again." Nonetheless, never again never ends.

I am not categorically labeling East Oakland or Compton as without life. What I am saying is that the gravest threats to black American community health do not move nor preoccupy the broader public. East Oakland is as far from adjoining communities as East Timor. Further, the effort to benefit black American communities by the government will not accomplish the goal. The conclusion being that the struggle continues for black Americans to rise to health and wealth from the ashes of slavery.

* * *

The American Civil Liberties Union (ACLU) put out an extensive readable article on the multitude of reasons the death penalty is a negative construct for the present day. The article, entitled, "The Case Against the Death Penalty," among other facts, lists as rationales for abolishing the death penalty: the irreversibility of executions, racial biases in sentencing, the excessive cost, and the false premise that the death penalty acts as a deterrent against crime. To the ACLU's list, I would add the effort of the condemned to redeem themselves in their own eyes and the eyes of society.

All human rights are first founded on the principle of life. Honoring life as sacred is a gateway for peace as it is constructive. If we base our thoughts on the inalienable right to life, we will orient ourselves toward life's preservation, resulting in a reevaluation of the causes and solutions for social ills that bring forth death or a death-bent mentality. Holding the principle that life is sacred will guide us out of the darkness that has clouded our collective understanding of right and wrong.

* * *

California death row is divided between an honor section, North Segregation, and a general section, East Block. Johnny Miles is housed in East Block, where there is no tier mingling. The men on East Block are let out of their cells strictly to be moved to another destination, such as the yard, the showers, the law library, or a visit. The men in North Segregation can mingle with each other freely on their tier for hours every day. There are minimal programs on death row, meaning, unlike the mainline, death row inmates have only religious services and yard exercise time as an opportunity to develop and rehabilitate themselves.

Most condemned men opt to live; however, living with a sense of purpose and positivity requires a program. A program is the activities and structure by which an inmate occupies himself. Programs generally include exercise, an intellectual outlet, and a spiritual practice. A further benefit to an inmate's program is pen-friends and people to call on the telephone. Speaking in broad strokes, outside friends benefit the inmate by providing an additional form of socialization, the satisfaction of being cared for, and a means for activity in the day.

For death row inmates, outsides friends often are persons that come from vastly different backgrounds, education, culture, race, and worldview. In a sense, death row inmates encounter the idealization of American society while in prison, in that a diversity of persons reach out with care and concern for a 'neighbor' who looks not like them and with a life experience unlike theirs. In this way do the inmates experience something similar to the "Beloved Community" in that despite differences, connections are made, and despite inequalities, there is not shaming of the poor, the inmate, but generosity in time, material, and heart are extended. Relationships of this sort benefit the condemned inmate as we should expect.

Here, let me address negativity or hate on death row. Such men and women are not in my circles, or those in my circles have not shown me that side of themselves. Hearing of murders, suicides, and drug overdoses occurring with frequency on California's Death Row attests to the reality and the prevalence of hate and inner-pain which most people would assume.

* * *

In "My History as a Collage Artist," Johnny Miles explains how he came to learn of the art of collaging. Collages and the art of collaging were unknown to Johnny before he entered death row. Johnny describes how a young person extended care to him through a letter and a collage. At the time he was in the adjustment center (AC), the hole, and using the given limited resources, he had to improvise a means for trying his hand at collaging. He had to find magazines and a way to cut and fasten images to paper. He did so even in the hole and when released to the mainline Johnny continued.

Johnny Mile's collage art is the diamond produced through nearly twenty-seven years of impaction by a solitary cell on death row, his own thoughts, and perceptions of self, and his character and propensities. Death row shaped Johnny Miles into a collage artist. Inspiration struck his person in the form of an adolescent's after-school letter to a death row inmate; he tried collaging and it worked for him. Since that day in 2003, Johnny Miles has been dedicated to the art form. Johnny Duane Miles, neighbor to the Bloods gang, privy to the culture of Niggas with Attitudes, condemned murderer and rapist, with a personality likely high on the psychopathy chart found purpose on death row that swings his thoughts to the highest human concepts. He has found his "in-mind" monastery and he is said to be constantly at work.

If all things are made to grow productive given the right circumstances, we can certainly try to understand why things became negative for a person or a people. Our society is increasing in sophistication. Ways of being and inherent characteristics of persons, such as same-sex (homosexual) and transgender identities, are finding face whereas in previous epochs such persons were subverted and thwarted. The balance between inherent character and behavior is finding a new middle ground. Right and wrong certainly exist yet in today's world there is less social or communal guidance as far as how to navigate between truth and falsehood for the reaching of self-actualization. We are in a time of intense debate, to the extent that the sun is arguing with the moon as to who is most needed. The truth is that they are both required for life to continue, but somehow that point is being forgotten.

There will be no social benefit to the people of California executing Johnny Miles. Johnny Miles is a convicted murderer in prison for life with universal approbation given the circumstances of his conviction. Out of harm's way, we can learn from him.

For my behalf, this book intends to honor the fight for life.

Tio MacDonald

March 2019

PART I
JOHNNY DUANE MILES

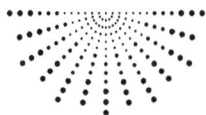

BIOGRAPHY

I, Johnny Duane Miles, was born at Torrance Memorial Hospital, in Torrance California in the year 1966, the month of December, on the day of the 12th. My parent's names are John Lewis Miles and Jean Patricia Holloway Miles. My father was a belt sander and my mother was a housewife. In the early 70's I attended kindergarten at Kelly Elementary, in the city of Compton, California.

My parents, three sisters, and I, in the mid-'70s, moved to Los Angeles, California. There I attended Woodcrest Elementary. Not long after, my parents moved us back to Compton. We moved to a different location in Compton, so I was enrolled in a different elementary school. Now I was enrolled in Foster Elementary, where I attended for the second grade. The year was 1974. I attended Foster Elementary through the 6th grade.

After graduating from Foster Elementary, in the year 1978, I then enrolled in Whaley Junior High School. My parent's home was close to the school. Frailey Avenue sat just across the main highway, Rosecrans, from Whaley Jr. High. It was a skip and a hop for me to attend.

I completed all 3 grades: 7th, 8th, and 9th. Graduating in 1982. I then enrolled in Dominguez High School, which I attended one day before checking out to enroll in Lynwood High School. I played basketball throughout my freshman year, which was a success.

My sophomore year wasn't such a success. I started getting into fights, so I decided to check out and check back into Dominguez High School. I attended for a few months, and even tried to get back into basketball, but due to foot surgery, I felt a step behind in basketball. Additionally, I was unable to focus on class work. This was around the year 1983.

During this time, I dropped out of high school to attend a continuation school, though I never attended any classes or walked into any classroom at all. I put myself in the streets, making fast money, and getting into trouble with the law.

Soon, I found myself facing some serious time for several alleged juvenile crimes. With no support system in place, I became prey to the courts and penal system. With due process being violated, I was sent off to the belly of the beast.

Without a clue of my future, in the year of 1985, in the belly of the beast, I wound up attending school, doing vocational jobs, and later laboring at fire camp. I became eligible for early parole November of 1987. Before paroling, while in fire camp, I meet a young lady, which led to the both of us courting each other through letters. With that said, once I was free from incarceration we decided to get married.

Free, married, and with a printing job, it's now the year of 1988. Work was good; it paid the bills. Wife was working. Smiles and laughter were at their best. Come 1989, we welcomed a baby daughter. We were in jubilation and the future looked bright.

Soon after I decided I would like to go back to school to pursue higher education with basketball being the route to make that happen. My wife agreed. I enrolled in Harbor Community College, located in San

Pedro, California. We also relocated to the Long Beach area, so that we could be closer to the school. The hard part of this arrangement was that my wife had to drive quite some distance to work, from Long Beach to Riverside County.

After 3 to 4 months in Long Beach, my wife decided to move back to Riverside. She felt frustrated due to the long drive to work, and the time we were now spending apart. She took my daughter with her. Such a move put distance in our relationship. Focusing on school became impossible.

Feeling at that time that California had been such a burden on me, for so long, and in many different ways, I decided to leave California and go to Atlanta, Georgia. It's early 1990. Within a few months, due to family issues, I left Atlanta to return to California.

Back in California, now dealing with family matters, I wound up moving in with my wife. It's still 1990. I get a job and things go swell, but family issues again were distancing our relationship, to where irreconcilable differences lead to us separating, then divorcing.

1991 – 1992: divorce papers filed. Now living in Compton California, working low and high-end jobs. I filed a multimillion-dollar lawsuit against the company I was working for. I enrolled in a vocational college, taking up: "Travel and Tourism" curriculum.

While visiting the city of Torrance, on a school assignment, my truck was hit with a barrage of bullets by the Torrance police. I was surely blessed that I lived through it. Once again, I found myself without a support system in place. Like before, I became prey to the police, the courts, etc: accused of heinous crimes, led to more accusatory crimes, which remain to this day.

Vindictively sentenced in one county, because I was vindictively sought in another: injustice spun it's wheel. After one dismissal in a death penalty case, it was soon refiled; after much continuance, injustice came to an unjust end: a persecution accentuated by death. In the absence of any direct evidence against my innocence, strangely enough, no picture could be falser than that which prevailed in my conviction. I proclaim my innocence.

From 1993 to 2000, I lived under constant harassment by the prosecutors and courts in the county of San Bernardino, West Valley Detention Center, where conditions were really rough. Having been oppressed by the lawgivers, I was shipped off to San Quentin, where I've been waiting for my appeals to process, which has been going on from 2000 to 2018. Prison is hardly a way of life for a family man. I vow to keep seeking freedom.

In art, I found a community life; with community acceptance, there came the further stimulus to dream and fantasize, seek education, and general self-improvement. Collaging prepared me for the experience of travel and enabled me to find friends. Through winds and currents extremely difficult for navigation I have navigated thus far. It's indeed an honor and privilege to participate in such a positive endeavor, of showing my collages and writings.

Given the opportunity, you'll come to know more about me, my art, my imprisonment, and future. It has been an incredibly challenging undertaking thus far. I shall survive.

MY PROCESS

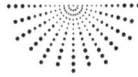

I have long poured my heart into collaging. When I sit down to start creating a collage, a philosophical light switches on in my head. There has never been a time, since the beginning of my creating collages, not once, the thought of rethinking the passion that was created, and that continues even on a higher passion to this day. With interest, everyone one of my collages takes on a life of its own, with a heartbeat. When I see that they do aid folks with a smile and conversations, my purpose was stamped, signed, and delivered. I feel that when I'm doing my work, my work is doing me. Creativity begets creativity...

MY HISTORY AS A COLLAGE ARTIST

When I was in the hole, which is called the AC (Adjustment Center), here at San Quentin Prison, I received a letter from a young inspiring student, who was a member of the Boys and Girls Club of the Bay Area. It was the year 2003. In the envelope, her letter read that she wanted to become a humanitarian, and travel to Africa, and other continents. Her goals warmed my heart, but it was what came next that propelled my mind. Within the same envelope was a collage she had created, her words told me so. At that time, I've never heard the word "collage" or viewed any works of the art (collaging). I do know her collage gave me a smile, then moved me deeply.

Being in the hole with nothing to do but read and write, a lightbulb went off in my head; the thought of making a collage of my own became ideal. I acquired a few magazines and paper, but I wasn't allowed glue, so gluing was out. It came to me to try tape, since I was able to stock pile tape from the canteen boxes they'd give us when canteen was delivered. I used a playing card, which was flat, for cutting. These items served my purpose, as I delved to commence to see where collaging would take me. Surprisingly enough, the first of them turned out fine.

Miraculously I was released from the hole, to my prison status changed. Now, I had the privilege of ordering glue, which I did so. From that point on, moving forward, collaging has become my heart, and has given me a place to grow.

When I look back, I can truly say I thank that young lady. She definitely has a humanitarian soul. Her collage has become every bit of all I've created. I am a branch growing from her tree. Now it is the year 2018, and collaging is still my lavished support; it has kept me strong. Collaging has been loyal to me, so I'll continue being loyal to collaging.

MY METHOD

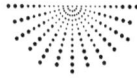

It helps to have four huge boxes of a variety of magazines; the majority of them I've pulled apart over the years. In preparing for creating a collage, I'll go through a pile I've accumulated, that may provide a starting point. Most of the time the theme is depicted within the scene of a page. If not, I'll create a theme. Then the arrangements come into play. I'll find the other pieces that are of interest, to the theme at hand. Some pieces have to be cut out, and this is where it gets tricky, because I am not allowed to have a razor or scissors. I discovered that inside earbuds (headphones), there's a little round aluminum piece that functions as a cutter for me. It works well.

I lay every piece out; then on the paper where I will glue them down on, I identify where each piece best fits. If the fit doesn't work, I'll have to go digging, searching for a right fit. Sometimes that can take a long time.

Using a small plastic gizmo, I apply a dab of glue onto the plastic gizmo and then apply the glue to the underside of each piece as I lay the pieces in place.

Following the path above is pretty much my routine for creating my collages. It helped when the generous gave me magazines to continue creating my art.

MY OVERVIEW EXPLANATION OF THE
SET OF COLLAGES IN THE BOOK

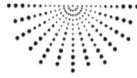

The collection of collages here are of an extended period of time, representing my commitment and respect for the arts. They were ignited by many different constructions, that were raised here in prison, and outside of these prison walls: education, politics, religion, economics, relationships, sports, and hopes, etc. I feel that this collection emerges together as a mindful flow, championing my creativity, and the world as a whole. They represent us all in growth.

PART II
LEARNING CURVE: POETRY &
COLLAGE OVERVIEWS

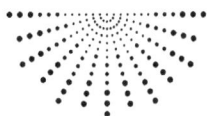

1

RAPID RISE

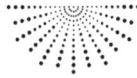

*I*magine the existence of tragedies

Could be pushed out of existence

Homicides meeting the same fate

The Earth would become a bumpy smooth place

It would be an increased gain

All corruption exiting the game

War changing it's name

Everyone free from blame

Drugs and alcohol fated the same

As tragedies and homicides

Non-existing in a Rapid Rise

I know it's exceedingly rare

People to ever think me to ever sit in a Rapid Rise chair

But picture me there

Being greeted like a bumpy smooth star

Push "N" my agenda far beyond bars

Because I'm addicted to the rights that's ours

That is...

Living large!

There's wisdom in my rhythm

As a new love for justice

When there's no justice

It goes far beyond than just us

They say increase your gains

Lesson your stay

There's more to live for

Outside of those prison gates

If you are to carry on...

Do so!

RAPID RISE

Imagine the existence of tragedies
Could be pushed out of existence
Homicides meeting the same fate
The Earth would become a bumpysmooth place
It would be an increased gain
All consumption exiting the game
War changing its name
Everyone free from blame
Drugs and alcohol fated the same
As tragedies and homicides
Now existing in a Rapid Rise
I know its exceedingly rare
People to even think to ever sit in
   a Rapid Rise chair
But picture me there
Being greeted like a bumpysmooth star
Pushin' my agenda far beyond bars
Because I'm addictive to the rights that's
   ours
That is ...
Living large !

There's wisdom in my Rhythm
As a new love for justice
When there's no justice
It goes far beyond than just us
They say increase your gains
Lesson your stay
There's known to live for
Outside of those prison gates
If you are to carry on ...
Do so !

By Johnny D. Miller
May 28, 2017

COLLAGE OVERVIEW - RAPID RISE

www.milesdynasty.com

"Rapid Rise" is the equal speed of anyone who ever imagined setting out to live an ideal utopian life.

The Rapid Rise lettering started off my process; then, I set the other pieces: [Upper Left] me in the studio, [Bottom Left] a record on a turntable, and [Upper Right] a rolling chair with a mountain scene view sitting within.

Being able to place myself in the studio, as well as having the keyhole, which flourishes with the mountain scene, my imagination surged to the height of every soul, that ever imagined a perfect world. That is to say, to keep moving, despite the world that we live in now!

(When we imagine, we create excellent potentials beyond the practical.)

After gluing down Rapid Rise to a sheet of paper, I searched for the other pieces, which took some time, because I had to browse through a couple of boxes of pulled apart magazines: First, I found the studio scene; then, I replaced the original face with mine, as if it is I who appears in the studio; subsequently, I came up with the keyhole sitting on the chair and I found the mountain view to place inside the keyhole; finally, I discovered the record playing on a turntable.

I finished Rapid Rise much faster than the usual, in a few hours. Sometimes, it may take all day just to find the needed pieces for a particular collage.

2

THE BATTLE FOR HEARTS AND MINDS

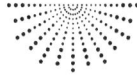

It is not effortless

When one accomplishes something grand

Woman or man

Free or in prison

Obstacles cannot crush us

A cultivated plan

The concept of genius in every aspect

Which is the ingredient of the next step

Intellect

Where artistry soar

No matter the challenge

Because we started from the bottom floor

Well as going back out of those revolving doors

In search for clues of our extraordinary futures

Where good fortune

Promise and opportunity collide

Within the triangle universe we view with our eyes

The battle for hearts and minds

Here is where we climb...

THE BATTLE FOR HEARTS AND MINDS

It is not effortless
when one accomplishes something grand
Woman or man
Free or in prison
Obstacles cannot crush us
A cultivated plan
The concept of genius in every aspect
which is the ingrediance of the next step
Intellect
Where artistry soar
No matter the challenge
Because we started from the bottom floor
Well as going back out of those revolving doors
In search for clues of our extraordinary futures
where good fortune ...
Promise and opportunity collide
Within the triangle universe we view with our eyes
The battle for hearts and minds
there is where we climb ...

By Johny D. Wilder
FEB/2018

COLLAGE OVERVIEW - THE BATTLE FOR HEARTS AND MINDS

www.milesdynasty.com

It was the sight of the heart being operated on [Left Corner], and the brain, focusing within a cosmic universal polygon [Top Middle], which influenced me to entitle this piece, "The Battle for Hearts & Minds."

Both heart and mind serve as a beacon, for the institutionalized studies of humanity, which every now and then, will cause a structural reform within societies. Such elated intellectual properties are definitely battled for.

Meanwhile, the institutional facility [Left Corner], with a vibrant shining moon high in the darkened sky, I'd imagine being a facility for the scholarly minds, to gather together, to battle out the understandings of the elected intellectual properties that cross their radar scopes.

The heart shaped piano, with student and teacher [Top Right], represent the attempt to increase the merger of intellectual knowledge, from adult to youth, musically, which also represents, the many musical themes within the battle for hearts & minds.

The inland view [Right Upper Side] represents the divided societies (different schools of knowledge) respectively.

[Lower Middle] The gentleman is climbing the steps towards the well-known schools for the elites, which were already proposed for him, and others, to attend before birth.

The drum set [Bottom Right] is the performing heartbeat of this piece, which is intended for echoing across the cosmic universal polygon.

The time to complete The Battle for Hearts and Minds was under 30 minutes, but the time seemed to extend because of the intellectual properties. It was as if I was truly focused within the cosmic universal polygon!

3
IN EED

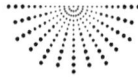

I need not to be weary in the confined space of my cell

But I do

Just the stress of living among so many alleged convicts

Who are facing execution

Myself included

Is wearisome

I need to never be distraught outside the reach of words

I need to be somewhere in the middle of my center at all times (focused)

I need very valuable growth

I need to console the living

I need the tools to be successful

When or if

Or if and when I return to the mainline

The community or beyond

The golden gates of heaven

I fully need to learn and come to understand the distinctions of existentialism...

I need

IN EED

I need not to be weary in the confined
    space of my cell

But i do

Just the stress of living among so many
    alleged convicts

Who are facing execution

Myself included

Is wearisome

I need to never be distraught outside the
    Reach of words

I need to be somewhere in the middle of
    my center at all times (Focused)

I need many valuable growth

I need to console the living

I need the tools to be successful

When or if

Or if and when i Return to the mainline

The community or beyond

The golden gates of heaven

I fully need to learn and come to understand
    the distinctions of existialism...

I need

By Johnny D. Wiles
Oct. 2016

COLLAGE OVERVIEW - IN EED

www.milesdynasty.com

By working within the shadow of "In EED," I've come to embrace various forms of strengths, to make efficient use of while living on the condemned row: dialoguing, writing letters, hobbying, hoping, and dreaming.

In EED has become my in-mind monastery. In EED is to exist efficiently daily, mediating on the endless events of my circumstances and survival.

Since its creation, In EED has put me in touch with my deeper thoughts, generating the spirit of positivity. By using its means, my spirits are lifted, thematized, methodically described, and analyzed. All pillared-on reason.

This work opened up a world for me. The monastery had drawn my mind free from prison, to its sanctuary. I thought, "What would it be like to experience In EED from the inside?"

Between the monastery and me, a transformation was born. I felt the vital energy of freedom. I identified myself as the man in the cave for the first time in years experiencing sunlight, after being stranded in darkness.

4

WHERE THE GOOD BECOME BAD AND
THE BAD BECOME GODS

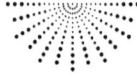

*H*eld captive by the courts persuasion and force

But the final battle is God's supernatural support

Well as the locale and international calls

Within and beyond these prison walls

It's up to you and I to illuminate our roles

To annihilate the ambitious and cultural killing machines of Death Row

As living creatures we must grow

Let's put death in a spaceship and send it back through the black hole

And dare it to never ever return

And let it be a lesson to be learned

For the upper level

Lower level

Ground level

So they can join the creative stir of no more burials

No evils

No needles

No injustices

They say we're in the times of when the horns are about to blow

Then God's seekers will take the world stage

To live out their lives in the original way

I picture heavens gates!

WHERE THE GOOD BECOME BAD
AND THE BAD BECOME GODS

Held captive by the courts persuasion and force
But the Finale battle is God's Supernatural
 Support
Well as the locale and international calls
Within and beyond these prison walls
It's up to you and I to illuminate our Roles
To annihilate the ambitions and cultural killing
 Machines of death Row
As living creatures we Must grow
Let's put death in a space ship and send it
 back through the black hole
And dare it to never ever to Return
And let it be a lesson to be learned
For the upper level
Lower level
Ground level
So they can join the creative stir of no
 More burials
No evils
No needles
No injustices
They say we're in the times of when the
 horns are about to blow
Then God's seekers will take the world
 stage
To live out their lives in the original way
I picture heavens gates!

By Johnny O. Wiles
Feb. 18, 2018

COLLAGE OVERVIEW - WHERE THE GOOD BECOME BAD
AND THE BAD BECOME GODS

www.milesdynasty.com

From the pinnacle heights of death row, a serum called, "Where the Good become Bad and the Bad become Gods" is being injected into the veins of society.

Venting feelings, expressing decisions, and influencing attitudes away from all fabrics of evil has been a monumental task. By attempting to remove the continuous causes of evil, nations have become strained and divided, unable to see the freshest (evergreen) point of living: existing in a non-murderous world.

Where the Good become Bad and the Bad become Gods was originally designed to encourage spiritual debates and spiritual deliberations on the matter of life and death.

I was exploring the vial [Center], like an open wound. The thought of liquefying the issues surrounding the death penalty came to mind; turning the issues into a chemical element: (Good = Bad); the arbitrary and capricious way of handing out the death penalty; the methods of obtaining illicit execution drugs; the operational methods of carrying out an execution; the uncertainties of the courts ever being fair or the courts executing an innocent person, etc.

The superior product of consciousness that is to be offered from the issues above certainly should be convincing in the reasons to avoid becoming a functional state murderer.

All the other pieces surrounding the vial, represent the time beyond the freshman, sophomore, junior, and senior years on death row.

5

DEADLY CONNECTIONS

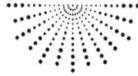

When I was a kid

And when I became aware of death

I said to myself

I wanted to live forever

Now as an adult

I'm profoundly uncomfortable with death

Death row has become my lecture on death

Death is fluent in all languages

The best way I describe death is operational

Rather than inspirational

The uninspirational element of death has motivated me to take action

Where to draw the line

I ask within my mind

Does death have an influential family?

Does death have a mother and father?

What would be some of its relatives names?

The notoriety death receives

Tilt the scales of being tamed

Trained for human use

Who would death like to see dead next?

I don't have to tell you that death is a problem

You already know

In fact death was instigated throughout the civil wars

Well as knocked on many nations doors

Created many riots in our times

And many accidents of many kinds

Death isn't soft spoken

Or mild mannered

But has many asperities

It is said the unveiling of the apocalypse will be its enemy

Then the parallels of death will end there

I'm with hope...

That my hope won't be strange fruit

For I know

I'm not or will not be

The Frankenstein they have stereotyped on me

This is my "Deadly Connections" anthropology

And I remind you

Experience doesn't come free!

DEADLY CONNECTIONS

When I was a kid
And when I became aware of death
I said to myself
I wanted to live Forever
Now as an adult
I'm profoundly uncomfortable with death
Deathrow has become my lecture on death
Death is fluent in all languages
The best way I describe death is operational
Rather than inspirational
The uninspirational element of death has
    Motivated me to take action
Where to draw the line
I ask within my mind
Does death have an influential family?
Does death have a mother and Father?
What would be some of its Relatives names?
The Notoriety death Receives
Tilt the scales of being tamed
Trained For human use

Who would death like to see dead next?
I don't have to tell you that death is a problem
You already know
In fact death was instigated throughout the
  civil wars
Well as knocked on many nations doors
Created many riots in our times
And many accidents of many kinds
Death isn't soft spoken
Or mild mannered
But have many asperities
It is said the unveiling of the apocalypse
  will be its enemy
Then the parallels of death will end there
I'm with hope ...
That my hope won't be strange fruit
For I know
I'm not or will not be
The Frankenstein they have stereotyped
  on me
This is my "Deadly Connections"
  anthropology

2

And I Remind you
Experiences doesn't come free!

By Johnny D. Wilks
OCTOBER / 2017

COLLAGE OVERVIEW - DEADLY CONNECTIONS

www.milesdynasty.com

The picture of Frankenstein commissioned my creative juices, leading to the creation of "Deadly Connections."

After acquiring the bold black letters for the title – Deadly Connections – the other pieces came along providing me the ability to manifest my vision for this collage. Shortly thereafter, I was gluing them together like a puzzle.

[Top Right Corner] A picture representing one of many civil wars, which have a deadly connection.

[Middle Right Side] The apocalyptic men on horseback, who will come to bring an end to all the ends of evil, which will have a deadly connection.

[Bottom Right Side] Deadly connections deposited by civil unrest, one of many riots, due to the looting of justice.

[Bottom Right Corner] An overturned automobile, wrecked by deadly connections, which seem to increase yearly.

[Bottom Left] Hope on a rope, in a dreary nightmarish field represents the kingdom of evil. This kingdom decreases freedoms on every level, when activated by a deadly connection charge.

[Upper Left Corner] The charge is induced by the evil hands. The charge sparks the prongs on the sides of Frankenstein's neck, which, in turn, release the monster of death upon corporations and society, depicted graphically on the RASTER on Frankenstein's face.

We may just have to wait for the apocalyptic men on horseback, to come along and put an end to all of the evils in the nightmarish field and replace the hope on the rope.

6

IMBUED

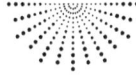

*a*round the clock

Two decades and a half

Right through

24 hours

Day after day

Many have come to walk this way

No!

I'm not talking about heaven's gates

I'm talking about incarceration's captivity

Yes!

The penitentiary

Some may meet justice half way

And receive an early release

But Kats like me are up against the two-headed beast

Which is:

The bias laws and the bias systems

Who hands down the ultimate sentences

Which seems like their secondary religions

The denominations of:

Life'ism • LWOP'ism • Death'ism

To defeat'em

One must hire a boss lawyer

Then out live'em

I give thanks to those who have led the way

Knowing it could be a short or long stay

Get educated

Choices and approbations

Doing time is no vacation

It's life's truth value vocational course

Humbly imbued to the core

Which seeds the experience

And more...

IMBUED

Around the clock

Two decades and a half

Right through

24 hours

Day after day

Many has come to walk this way

No!

I'm not talking about heaven's gates

I'm talking about incarceration's captivity

Yes!

The penitentiary

Some may meet justice half way

And receive an early Release

But Kats like me are up against the two headed
beast

Which is :

The bias Laws and the bias systems

who hands down the ultimate sentences

Which seems like their secondary
religions

The denominations of :

Life'ism · LWOP'ism and Death'ism

To definition

One must hire a bias Lawyer

Then out livem

I give thanks to those who have lead the
way

Knowing it could be a short or long stay

Get educated

All that we come to know

Choices and appreciations

Doing time is no vacation

Its life's truth value vocational course

Humbly imbued to the core

which seeds the experience

And more ...

By Johnny D. ___

COLLAGE OVERVIEW - IMBUED

www.milesdynasty.com

When one becomes impregnated with a strong sense of duty, one's heart becomes filled with joy, to perform, to achieve, to carry out plans. Being so "imbued" gives great satisfaction, to see oneself growing toward living a full life, with varying details.

I was reading a chapter out of a book, I believe to be entitled: "II/Freedom." I was only given Chapter 6 of that book, which was about responsibility. I came across a quote referring to Jean-Paul Sartre. It went like this:

"Sartre's view of freedom is far reaching: the human being is not only free but is doomed to freedom. Furthermore, freedom extends beyond being responsible for the world (that is, for imbuing the world with significance): one is also entirely responsible for one's failures to act."

I hope that this collage promotes many to action, by having a great impact, toward the world's continuous growth, positively.

7

A LOADED GUN

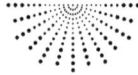

The many threats a loaded gun imposes is astronomical

Surely part of the solution depends on who you're asking

Some say guns are a direct threat to their survival

On the other hand

Some say it's a direct need

Then they read off their constitutionality

It's become(s) very challenging to generate empathy

To change hearts and minds about guns has an extensive history

We have the economic and cultural factors to consider

In the middle of this path you have the heavy hitters

This kind of connection only gets bigger

It ain't hard to figure

Who has their finger on the trigger

Just count the bodies in the storage room freezer.

A LOADED GUN

The many threats a loaded gun imposes is
astronomical

Surely part of the solution depends on who
you're asking

Some say guns are a direct threat to
their survival

On the other hand

Some say its a direct need

Then they read off their constitutionality

It's become(s) very challenging to generate empathy

To change hearts and minds about guns has
an extensive history

We have the economic and cultural
factors to consider

In the middle of this path you have
the heavy hitters

This kind of connection only get's bigger

It ain't hard to figure—

Who has their finger on the—
trigger

Just count the bodies in the storage
room freezer

By Johnny D. Miles
Feb / 2018

COLLAGE OVERVIEW - A LOADED GUN:

www.milesdynasty.com

With all the gun issues presently before us, open fire rings in my head, ricocheting within my skull! Crouching inside my brain is the thought of survival, of trying to survive.

The words, "A Loaded Gun" [Left Corner] provide me with the eerie musical sound of pistols [Below a Loaded Gun] running for their lives, screaming, "Guns don't kill people! We can't even pull our own triggers!" But the bigger figure, meaner than an AR-15 [Center] screams to the running pistols, "Kill that noise! Kill that noise! It's me that they want to put to rest, but it's not that easy! Its more political than your little running feet will ever know! As long as that little so-called meaningful action of the Second Amendment stands, it will always be 'us vs. them!'"

[Upper Right Corner] Fixed with an evil eye, death stares down the barrel, from within a pistol. Evil has dispensed out death since long gone centuries, long before the fingers of today, place theirs upon the trigger: mindset of the past vs. mindset of today.

[Lower Right Corner] The answer is always, "Yes!" when it comes to the saying: "Monkey see monkey do!"

The fallen figures [Lower Left Corner] represent the many folks that have died by the bullet.

I would like for you to imagine with me the eerie musical sound of running pistols. I imagine it would be bluuuesy!

8

WITHOUT THE SOUL

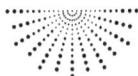

*W*ithout the soul

There's no harmony

Or pre-establishment with the body

Or all the representations of one

And the same universe

Without the soul

All is aphasia

To say

The loss of the power to use

Or understand words

Fails the absolute

The ultimate

The all embracing

The unconditional reality

Within an infinite existence of diversity

Without the soul

There could not be an admittance of my collagical poetry

We are driven by our souls

Without our souls

We can't fly

Or roll...

Down the unlimited boundaries of the soul

WITHOUT THE SOUL

Without the soul
There's no harmony
Or pre-establishment with the body
Or all the Representations of one
And the same universe
Without the soul
All is aphasia   (ə fā'zhə)
To say
The loss of the power to use
Or understand words
Fails the absolute
The ultimate
The all embracing
The unconditional Reality
Within an infinite existence of diversity
Without the soul
There could not be an admittance of
    My Collagical poetry
We are driven by our souls
Without our souls
We can't fly
Or Roll...

Down the Unlimited boundaries
    of the soul

By Johnny D. Niles
July/2017

COLLAGE OVERVIEW - WITHOUT THE SOUL

www.milesdynasty.com

I sit pouring over everything that exists in my environment, that either attracts or affects me positively or negatively. I believe it would be impossible for me to understand anything, let alone the many complexities of life, without the soul.

I believe the soul to be the "Knowing."

By being driven by my soul, I've represented many schools of philosophy and many other schools of knowledge as well.

Without the Soul:

[Bottom Right Corner]

The roads of life that I've traveled.

[Lower Left Corner & Upper Right Corner]

The aircraft is related to me seeing and understanding things on a higher plane, within and outside of my mind.

[Top Left Corner]

The bridge I've crossed from the past moving forward into present time.

[The Red Car]

My body driven by my Soul.

[Below the Red Soul]

My brain which is the engine of my body.

[Above the Red Soul]

A place in my mind I call, "Tranquility Contemplation" – my understanding zone.

The intellectual properties entailed in "Without the Soul" are to be studied, and you are now a passenger.

To be continued...

9

FAITH

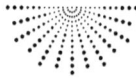

(WHAT IS IT?)

Faith is the assured expectation of what is hoped for: the evident demonstrations of realities that are not seen

Faith is believing that one will receive the witness that one has pleased God well

Faith is by keeping the memory of the place from which one has departed, one shall have the opportunity to return

Faith is the Lord dwelling in one's heart with love

Faith is having faith in God

Faith is being in union with the Lord

Faith is subjecting oneself to the righteousness of the Lord

Faith is thanking the Lord unceasingly

Faith is praying with holy spirit

Faith is believing in God's power, not men's wisdom

Faith is not doubting at all

Faith is of much greater value than gold

Faith is being rooted and built up in the Lord's wisdom

Faith is carrying on in a manly way

Faith is loving one's brothers and passing over from death to life

Faith is rejoicing with the truth

Faith is putting up a hard fight

FAITH
what is it?

Faith is the assured expectation of what is hoped for. the evident demonstration of realities that are not seen.

Faith is believing that one will receive the witness that one has pleased God well

Faith is by keeping the memory of the place from which one have departed, one shall have the opportunity to return

Faith is the Lord dwelling in one's heart with love

Faith is having faith in God

Faith is being in union with the Lord

Faith is subjecting oneself to the righteousness of the Lord

Faith is thanking the Lord unceasingly

Faith is praying with holy spirit

Faith is believing in God's power, not men's wisdom

Faith is not doubting at all

Faith is of much greater value than gold

Faith is being rooted and built up in the Lord's wisdom

Faith is carrying on in a manly way

Faith is loving one's brothers and passing over from death to life

Faith is Rejoicing with the truth
Faith is putting up a hard Fight

By Johnny D. Wiles
Feb/2018

COLLAGE OVERVIEW - FAITH (WHAT IS IT?)

www.milesdynasty.com

When I came across the theme, depicted in bold letters, as the center piece of this collage, "Faith: What is it?" I thought about the previous collage I entitled "Q & A." Then a minute or so later, I came across the image, "Questions & Answers" spelled out with a handheld magnifying glass, centered between the pages of an open book [Atop of Faith.] Intuitively, I felt compelled to respond to the question at hand: "Faith: What is it?"

My answer was: "Faith is asking to be named in the book of life, so that when one's time is up here on earth, one may go to live in paradise."

Until death, we press on by using the necessary tools [Below Faith], to chisel our names in the Book of Life.

First, one must enter into the contract that reads: "Basic instructions before leaving earth" – B.I.B.L.E. – and stick to the script, to be awarded.

The Map of Northern California [Below the Tools] represents the area of my and other like-minded believers' location. The motorcycle [Top Right] facing the flight of stairs, represents, the fierce work it takes to get to the stairway to Heaven. The rooftop steeple [Top Right Corner] represents the roof above Heaven's gates.

10

THE BOOK OF LIFE

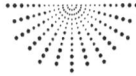

*M*y heart has become the pendulum of time

Past, present, and future

Pendulously swaying circuitously in their midst:

The midst of their divine attributes

The midst of their natural religion

The midst of their evolutionary epistemology

The midst of their scientific realism

So...as I cut through the very time of space!

I've set my sights on the greatest prize of all

To humble myself before my maker...

The book of life, expression found in Hebrew and Christian scriptures signifying a record kept by the Lord of those destined for eternal happiness (Exodus 32:32; Psalms 68; Malachi 3:16 Daniel 12:1; Philippians 4:3; Revelation 3:5, 17:8, 20:12, 21:27.)

THE BOOK OF LIFE

My heart has become the pendulum of time
Past, present and Future
Pendulously swaying circuitously in their mist:
The mist of their divine attributes
The mist of their natural Religion
The mist of their evolutionary epistemology
The mist of their scientific Realism
So... as I cut through the longtime of space!
I've set my sights on the greatest prize of all
To humble myself before my maker ...

The book of life, expression found in Hebrew
and christian scriptures signifying a record kept
by the Lord of those destined for eternal
happiness (Exodus 32:32; Psalms 68; Malachi 3:16;
Daniel 12:1; Philippians 4:3; Revelation 3:5, 17:8, 20:12,
21:27).

By Johnny D. Miller
January 2018

COLLAGE OVERVIEW - THE BOOK OF LIFE

www.milesdynasty.com

When I came across the phrase, "The Book of Life" new opportunities emerged from within my imagination.

As the Bible in acronym reads: "Basic Instructions Before Leaving Earth" (B.I.B.L.E.) I've given the Book of Life an acronym that reads: "Living in Festive Eternity" (L.I.F.E.)

We will welcome it as a book of remembrance and we all will have one, written from our affairs, and our life experiences.

The classroom setting [Flanking the Title] with black board, book shelf, and cluttered desk, represent the alignment between teaching and learning. Both teacher and learner would be perceptive of the massive fire swirling within the black hole along with the swinging, heart shaped, clock-pendulum [Center.] They represent the better parts of our past and present, advancing toward our festive eternity: the black hole will deliver us to our youth, to an eternity when wrongdoing does not exist.

11

VICTORY

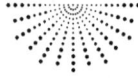

When we first met he spoke of his game with much confidence

I said to myself

If I had his game I could beat me every time

Old school and new school combined

His words were youthful vigor

I once aged down into his figures

With words of confidence just as mightier

Be it as the present time has allowed our acquaintance

Vigor and mightier have clashes like symbols on a drum set

A sound so beautiful

Beautiful as tennis shoes making the squeaky sound on a hardwood basketball court

My mind wonders

Where was his support?

As we play the game I listen, learn, teach

It's so hard not to preach

Most of the time not

I'd just think

And say

If I had his game I could beat me every time

Just as those who made and those who will create their history

We're still striving and struggling for victory

Striving and struggling for victory

Old school and new school combined

V I C T O R Y

VICTORY

When we first met he spoke of his game
    with much confidence
I said to myself
If I had his game I could beat me everytime
Old school and New school combined
His words were youthful vigor
I once aged down into his figures
With words of confidence just as mightier
Be it as the present time has allowed our
    acquaintance
Vigor and mightier has clashed like cymbals
    on a drum seat
A sound so beautiful
Beautiful as tennis shoes making the squeaky
    sound on a hardwood basketball court
My mind wonders
where was his support
As we play the game I listen. learn. teach
Its so hard not to preach
Most of the time not
I'd just think
And say
If I had his game I could beat me everytime
Just as those who made and those who will
    create their history
We're still striding and staggling for Victory
Striving and staggling for Victory
Old school and new school combined

V.
    i
        C
            T
                O
                    R
                        Y . . .

by Henry Dukes

COLLAGE OVERVIEW - VICTORY

www.milesdynasty.com

That performance! That high performance! That high performance delivered! Now that's Victory!!

That huge V [Off-Left Center] won my imagination, instantaneously. My mind electronically rose above, within the midst of the alphabet letters, spelling V-I-C-T-O-R-Y. All I could think about was an all net cash flow rising from the hardwood floor and I making moves as if I was in the NBA or NCAA.

Now that it's just a fantasy, dreams of being there never go away.

[Top-Right Corner] An engine which represents that fantasy of being in the NBA or NCAA. During basketball season it never cuts off. During off season that engine sometimes is idle.

12

THE RIGHT TOOLS (TRENDS)

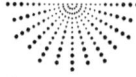

My incarceration will forever provoke curiosity about another time and place

Being within this institution remains another time and place unchanged

The right tools are a requirement for survival

As fortitude and discipline are critical to success

As passion and perseverance are the grit trends

That drive us to achieve

When we look back at our distant past

Oh do we welcome new ideas

We may see our past as an antique structure that has to be changed

So we start rebuilding

First by laying down a new foundation

But I remind you!

In this crazy hectic atmosphere

There's no days off in prison

However...with the right tools

We are at service to ourselves

And our communities

> Leonardo da Vinci once said: "Obstacles cannot crush me. He who is fixed to a star does not change in mind."

> Aristotle proposed that how one used one's property was an indicator of virtue.

THE RIGHT TOOLS (TRENDS)

My incarceration will forever provoke curiosity
about another time and place
Being within this institution remains another
time and place
unchanged
The Right tools are a requirement for survival
As fortitude and discipline are critical to
success
As passion and perseverance are the grit
trends
That drives us to achieve
When we look back at our distant past
Oh do we welcome new ideas
We may see our past as an antique structure
that has to be changed
So we start Rebuilding
First by laying down a new foundation
But I remind you!
In this crazy hectic atmosphere
There's no days off in prison
However ... with the Right tools
We are at service to ourselves
And our communities

Leonardo da Vinci, once said: "Obstacles cannot
crush me. He who is 'fixed to a star does not
change his mind".

Aristotle proposed that how one used one's
property was an indicator of virtue.

By Johnny D. Miles
Sept. 2017

COLLAGE OVERVIEW - THE RIGHT TOOLS (TRENDS)

www.milesdynasty.com

When the Right Tools are available, the many advantages of having them becomes apparent.

By bridging oneself over to and within the culture of tomorrow's leaders and creative trendsetters one is to be bathed in light. It gives me great satisfaction having read presently and formerly incarcerated author's inspirational memoirs—their life events and the changes they've made. Being suffused within their leadership gives me hope and a path to tread down. Real support.

Useful tools and building a culture, became the moment's reflection, as the title captained my thoughts. I became a player and a fan of this piece inevitably, and to pass it on, through the proper channels of trending, to those who will become immediate players and fans of this piece also, would surely be a sharing moment of added reflections.

13

Q & A

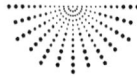

*T*he rhythms of my inextricable presence

The ebb and flow of my journey

Printed and sealed

My soul and nature are related within

Here is where the questions and answers begin

Q & A

Is part of my DNA

I ask questions

And want answers everyday

Which is so necessary

And timeless

Q + A

The rhythms of my inextricable presence

The ebb and flow of my journey

Printed and sealed

My soul and nature are related
within

Here is where the questions and
answers begin

Q and A

Is part of my DNA

I ask questions

And want answers everyday

Which is so necessary

And timeless

By Johnny D. Wilson
Feb/2015

COLLAGE OVERVIEW - Q & A

www.milesdynasty.com

Q & A is another justifiable title:

When I came across Q & A [Center], the letters stood out, significantly, as a symbol; a symbol applicable to every aspect of our lives, representing the questions and answers that have emerged via our universal curiosities from childhood through adulthood.

Within an hour after gluing down the Q & A, I generated all the other pieces:

The female and male construction workers, building the hundred-dollar bill, represent equal pay in the work force [Lower Left]. The ear [Bottom Left] is loving the sound of money constructionally being made. What's more are the many, many pies on saucer plates, which represent the question marks that are assigned to every aspect of our lives, when a question is posed. The bite of chocolate ice cream [Above Left], projects a love affair flourishing and savoring across questions and answers (Q & A opportunities.)

Having a fondness for whipped cream, polished nails, pearls and piles of money, a dream to be reckoned with, I propose a question: "Can a man of my stature achieve such things?"

I tastefully await the answer...

THE SPIN BEGINS

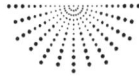

The reels of my dreams keep on spinning

Revolving colorfully,

More so when I'm asleep

That natural periodic suspension of my consciousness

Which trumps my wakefulness

So vividly endlessly

Dream versus reality

The choice of where I'd rather be

Truly reels no mystery

Lava melts away my condemnatory condition

Where lightening electrifies my mission

Sweet enough for sippin'

Continuously...

Under fur covers sweltering

With my significant other

So vividly endlessly

Dream versus reality

The choice of where I rather be

Where I'd rather be

Dreams becoming reality...

THE SPIN BEGINS

The feels of my dreams keep on spinning
Revolving Colorfully
More so when I'm asleep
That natural periodic suspension of my
    Consciousness

Which trumps my wakefulness
So vividly endlessly
Dream versus Reality
The choice of where I Rather be

Truly feels no mystery
Lava melts away my condemnatory condition
Where lightening electrifies my mission
Sweet enough for Sippin'

Continuously...
Under Fire Colors sweltering
with my significant other
So vividly endlessly

Dream versus Reality
The choice of where I Rather be
Where I Rather be
Dreams becoming Reality...

By Johnny D. Miles
Feb/2018

COLLAGE OVERVIEW - THE SPIN BEGINS

www.milesdynasty.com

It's happening more than ever, my dreams and fantasies are spinning from different sized multicolored projector reels [Left Corner.]

In essence, a favorite spin, on a romantic campaign, that's in a class of its own, invites the other pieces to make way for a potential future. We bond together in passion, sipping thunder and lightning, which gives reason enough to nurture, the hot steamy lava that comes next, that spans for miles.

I say to us all, it's never too late to start dreaming and fantasizing, because it will be well worth it for health and happiness. So start where the spin begins!

Also, I want to tell you how much it means to me to share with you my dreams and fantasies, so, likewise, never give up on yours. Let the multicolor reels play!

The spin begins really speaks for itself within my mind...now yours. Have a sip!

THE ORIGINAL

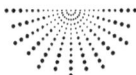

*H*ats fitted with style

Originating an inviting dreaminess

A place to meet and talk

To seek compromise and settle disputes

Within ideas blossom and bear fruit

Bridging differences and fostering unity

The original...ideology

It all started with good and evil in the Garden of Eden

So here we are

Here today

Good surviving something so bad

It just goes to show

We're built to last!

THE ORIGINAL

Hats fitted with style
Originating an inviting dreaminess
A place to meet and talk

To seek compromise and settle disputes

Within ideas blossom and bear fruit

Bridging differences and fostering unity

The Original ... ideology

It all started with good and evil in the Garden
of Eden

So here we are

Here today

Good surviving something so bad

It just goes to show

we're built to last!

By Johnny D. Miles
Feb 2018

COLLAGE OVERVIEW - THE ORIGINAL

www.milesdynasty.com

In an original way, many legends originated under many hats: politically, religiously, economically, socially, and musically.

By operating in accord with the hats, they set the main theme: "Original."

Surely, they are historically generated yet of infinite duration. Certainly, there was a divine mind behind them, and many great minds have worn their hats hence, bringing about the evolution of style and taste, for different societies.

I'm blissfully attached to such affairs!

As an aim, I am driven from the past to the present, jaunting back and forth. My mind rests on the principle, that we will have worn many kinds of hats, mentally and physically, throughout our lives. Hats on!

THE LEARNING CURVE

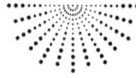

From the crowd of the condemned

    I catch sight of my own tortured soul

Crowded amongst them

Which is a waiting game

Until finally pawned over to death

Which the system prepares obsessively

From a long period kept

But many die from old age or bad health

Delirious suicides of some killing self

Dead and gone for decades

Are the death chambers escapades

The systems stomp their feet and dance

For the grim reaper to start up its theme song again

Medievalism poisonous let's shoot'em up with drugs!

Which is an incendiary for revenge

And if the grim reaper sing...

Many won't cringe

The debate will be up and running again

And if the end reach in

There's only one of two ends that could reach in:

The end of the death penalty

Or the killing machine is up and running again

And when then

How will it conscience?

THE LEARNING CURVE

From the crowd of the condemned
I catch sight of my own torchened soul
Crowded amongst them
Which is a waiting game
Until finally passed over unto death
Which the system prepares obsessively
From a long period kept
But many die from old age or bad health
Delirious suicides of some killing self

Dead and gone for decades
Are the death chambers escapades
The system stomp their feet and dance
For the grim reaper to start up its theme
    song again
Medievalism poisonous let's shoot 'em up with
    drugs!
Which is an incendiary for revenge
And if the grim reaper sing...
Many won't cringe
The debate will be up and running again
And if the end reach in
There's only one of two ends that could
    reach in
The end of the death penalty
Or the killing machine is up and running
    again
And when then
How will it conscience?

By Johnny D. Wilco
    Feb/2018

COLLAGE OVERVIEW - THE LEARNING CURVE

www.milesdynasty.com

Revising and adjusting are essential to the "Learning Curve."

Upon suitable reflection, one can achieve awareness in its genuine nature, so as to aim at and preserve the key lessons to one's experiences.

Within the Learning Curve my thoughts are punctuated by all the specifics surrounding the death penalty. I feel empowered by the Learning Curve, my Learning Curve, because of its sophisticated curving issues, presenting such complexities, as moratoriums, the voting in of proposition 66, and the speeding-up of executions. My understanding being had after many years.

(Even as death row gets a lot more crowded than it was even a couple of years ago...we're still just part of the crowd.)

Surprising revelations have been exposed about San Quentin's new execution chamber: it's cost, the procedures, the price of an execution when or if they ever will. There are numerous articles addressing the challenges facing lethal injections and the designs of the institutionalized industries of death. Yet still, is the all-important question of why not end the death penalty?

When a death sentence is reversed due to errors, mischief, and/or the miscarriage of justice, it not only removes the blindfold from the eyes of lady justice, but from our eyes as well. ("No, I am alive!")

The Learning Curve represents the surreal tranquility of my peace.

EAST OAKLAND TIMES

The East Oakland Times, LLC (EOT) is a multi-media publication based in the San Francisco Bay Area. Founded by chief editor, Tio MacDonald. EOT has at its core three principles: the principle of the dignity of life, the principle of liberty, and the principle of tolerance. EOT supports the flourishing of civilization through the peace found by honoring these three stated principles.

Current Projects Include:

- Publishing of the My Crime Series www.crimebios.com
- The Publication of Original Inmate Books
- Podcasts from California's Condemned Row (www. eastoaklandtimes.com or youtube/East Oakland Times)
- Print Publication for Free Distribution on the Streets of East Oakland
- Publication of EOT produced books on current topics, such as youth recidivism

By leaving a favorable review you encourage others to buy EOT produced books and thereby YOU support EOT's mission.

Support the EOT by purchasing EOT produced e-books, print books, and audiobooks!

EAST OAKLAND

www.ingramcontent.com/pod-product-compliance
Lightning Source LLC
Chambersburg PA
CBHW070642030426
42337CB00020B/4124